IT AIN'T OVER!

THREE LITTLE WORDS THAT LEAD TO PERSONAL AND PROFESSIONAL FULFILLMENT

Joyce E. Brooks

Books by Joyce E. Brooks:

Self-Inflicted Overload

It Ain't Over!

Joyce E. Brooks   *It Ain't Over!*
Copyright © 2014
96 pages

ISBN 978-0-692-29372-0

Printed in Montgomery, AL by Davis Direct
www.davisdirect.com

www.joyceebrooks.com

DEDICATION

Before May 28, 2014

Brooks, Jae and Matthew, in this life we all will experience good days and bad days. I pray you always have more good days than bad. Let your good days carry you through your bad days. And never forget: "It ain't over until you are six feet under."

Love unconditionally, stand strong, be good and stay true to yourself until the end. Love my boys with all my heart!!

After May 28, 2014

Brooks, I dedicate *It Ain't Over!* to you.

I had no idea of the full meaning of this title and the content of this book until now. I thank God for calling me to be Esther in your life. I thank you for giving me the honor and privilege to serve as your wife for 14 years.

Good Night.
Sweet Dreams.
Love You.
Until we meet again!

Joyce E.

CONTENTS

Resurrection – It's Never Over
>What do Mandela, Tiger, Jennifer, Auburn University and Ivor J. Brooks have in common?

PART III: NO EXCUSES

The Indictment of "Mr. Opportunity"
Confessions of a Recovered Pessimist
Succeeding Against the Odds
Collateral Damage
My Daddy
What Now? Spectator or Participant

Takeaways
From My Mother
Afterword
Bonus - It Ain't Over: The Spoken Word Version
>**I Am Who I Am**
>**Love, where are you?**

About Joyce E.
Acknowledgements

FOREWORD

*Success consists of going from failure to failure without
loss of enthusiasm.* ~ Winston Churchill

It Ain't Over! is a book for people striving for success in a myriad
of circumstances, situations and various aspects of life. Whether you
are seeking financial success, career success, success in relationships
or just being a better person, Joyce has found several ways to succeed
in life through her personal experiences – despite failures, missed
opportunities and, yes, even the devastating loss of "her best friend and
husband." Throughout her journey, Joyce never lost her enthusiasm for
life because: **It Ain't Over.**

I worked for Alabama Power for four decades and completed my
career as Senior Vice President and Chief Ethics Officer. I am an
engineer by training who ultimately, by the Grace of God, was placed
in a position to do the greatest good for the most people. That said, I
am certain Joyce E. Brooks is the real deal. She has developed a clear
and concise way to view any of life's experiences as opportunities.

Approximately two decades ago, Joyce made an appointment
to see me in my office in Mobile, Alabama. At that time she was an
engineering student at the University of South Alabama. It did not
take me long to recognize a highly intelligent young person with a
bright future. In addition, Joyce appeared to be much wiser than her
age at that time. She joined Alabama Power Company after graduating
from South Alabama and it was there that I observed her in various
situations, including, at times, very stressful circumstances. She never
allowed these circumstances – good or bad – to define who she was.

From my experience and perspective, this book is a must read. It's
written for anyone who desires to live a successful and fulfilling life
regardless of the temporary joy one experiences when they meet or
exceed a goal or the disappointment that follows when a perceived
missed opportunity has passed them over. Because of the genuineness

that comes across through her life experiences, Joyce's candor and openness is refreshing, insightful and provocative.

Finally, as I view this book in the context of Joyce's current situation, it is clear to me that God – Elohim – through the Holy Spirit was the inspiration and enabler for the writing of this profound message and the notion that **It Ain't Over**.

Joyce, to God be the glory for the things you have done and will do.

Robert Holmes
Retired Senior Vice President of Ethics, Alabama Power Company
Motivational speaker, mentor and ethics lecturer
June 2014

INTRODUCTION

Who doesn't want success? Success in your career. Success in your relationships. Success in raising your children. Success in your finances. Success in everything you pursue.

Defining success varies from person to person. The common strand between various perspectives of success is a desire to experience personal fulfillment. To say you are fulfilled indicates a feeling of happiness, satisfaction and accomplishment. In a state of fulfillment, what defines true success can be confidently determined by considering the goals, expectations, pursuits and achievements you have set for yourself.

Life is a series of experiences. Each experience can be defined by its own unique set of circumstances as well as its own unique outcomes. An opportunity can very well be the determining factor between success and failure. How will an actress become an Academy Award winner if she never had the opportunity to perform? How will a farmer have a plentiful harvest if he did not have the opportunity to own a farm? How will a child learn to love others if he never had the opportunity to be loved? Life experiences are often introduced by an opportunity. The success or failure of that opportunity is directly impacted by how hard one is willing to work to recognize the opportunity's potential.

An opportunity is a chance. It is a chance to succeed, achieve, fail, experience and realize a dream. More importantly, it is a chance to become your very best and live a more fulfilling life. Simply, an opportunity is a chance to *try*. When opportunity meets hard work, the possibilities are limitless.

The most common opportunities can be classified as golden, nonexistent, missed or undercover. I have had the pleasure and disappointment of each type of opportunity. Each experience brought its own set of circumstances, outcomes and lessons. One of the greatest lessons I've learned is that **"It Ain't Over!"**

There are times in life that a golden opportunity comes knocking at your door with clear, welcomed possibilities. What a pleasant surprise to have a golden opportunity seek you out for a job, promotion, relationship, investment or a new venture! There is much to be gained when a golden opportunity comes knocking. There is also a chance to *try*.

Conversely, it can be very disappointing and frustrating to wait for an opportunity to knock at your door. You may wonder: Did opportunity lose my address? You may begin to doubt yourself, your abilities and even the future. Opportunity seems nonexistent. What do you do when opportunity is knocking, but it just isn't knocking at your door?

What do you do when opportunity is knocking, but when you look out the window it's undoubtedly your worst nightmare? That's exactly what happened to me on Wednesday, May 28, 2014. My husband and best friend, Birmingham Fire Chief Ivor Jerome Brooks, Sr., met with his untimely death. *How could this be?* The draft of this book was complete. The editor of the draft, Carrie Banks, had completed the final review and e-mailed it back to me just days prior to May 28th. The graphic artist was finalizing the cover design.

On the morning of May 28th, I had just spoken to Robert Holmes about the timeline for the book release. Brooks and I had agreed that Robert should write the foreword. We also discussed when and where we should hold the book release party. I was only weeks away from celebrating the official release of my second book, ***It Ain't Over! Three Little Words that Lead to Personal and Professional Fulfillment.*** Instead, I found myself celebrating the life and legacy of Chief Ivor J. Brooks, Sr., as he transitioned to a higher calling. Brooks is dead. Yes, he is gone. He made his last run and received his last call.

I found myself momentarily lost without him, asking myself: *What am I supposed to do now?* Thank God there is something called the Holy Spirit to bring you through times of crisis, turmoil and tragedy. Looking back on those very difficult days, I realize I was also called on May 28, 2014, by a higher caller to a higher purpose. It was like I was a soldier in the Army – I signed up for service expecting to receive a salary and all the benefits but never imagined I would be deployed to go to Afghanistan, Iraq or the Gulf War. I received my official deployment orders May 28th. It was time for me to accept the assignment and perform my duties.

As his wife, friend and mother of his children, I had the honor and privilege of overseeing and assuring that his services were a celebration of life and not a day of mourning. I recognized that all were watching, especially my sons. It was my opportunity to demonstrate grace under fire.

When your opportunity appears to be a nightmare, this is not the time to have a pity party, assign blame or become discouraged. And it's definitely not the time to give up. When opportunity doesn't knock – or you *think* opportunity hasn't knocked – or opportunity appears as a nightmare – it's easy to do all these things and more. However, there are positive, productive steps that will lead to a better outcome. **First,** you must believe **"It Ain't Over!"** If we think and respond as if it's over ... guess what? **It *is* over!**

Initially, I was absolutely certain Brooks' death could **NOT** possibly be an opportunity. Yet, over the five days leading to the funeral on Monday, June 2, 2014, God showed me that Brooks' death was no mistake. The events, activities and unexpected actions of many during this crisis gave me an opportunity of a lifetime. I am humbled and honored that God saw fit to *allow* Satan to test every nerve, cell and fiber of my being.

As I write, I realize the test is not over – nor is my resolve to respond to these circumstances with Grace. The difficult days ahead will be met with my love, faith and trust in God to provide sustaining power. This power is for me, my family, loved ones and enemies as **everyone** who knew Chief Brooks is introduced to a new normal in the days ahead. The future isn't just about me.

****

Have you ever wondered what it is about one person and not another that invites opportunity to their door over and over and over again? Some people have all the luck. There was a time I felt the same way. I wondered what it was the "lucky" person possessed that I did not. What was the "lucky" person doing that I wasn't doing?

Perhaps, however, it wasn't luck. Could it possibly have been something a little more concrete and predictable? Maybe this "lucky" person recognized an opportunity even when it didn't look like one. Opportunities are often missed because they didn't arrive at the door perfectly packaged with a **"Guaranteed to Succeed"** label. Perhaps this person's "luck" was actually recognition!

Think about that co-worker who declined a new assignment because a promotion was not guaranteed. What about the popular girl who would not go out with the guy on the debate team because he dressed funny and wore thick glasses? What about the person who failed to speak up on behalf of the powerless because of fear of rejection or judgment?

In each case, an opportunity was missed. This type of opportunity can be labeled as "under cover". It was well concealed. It was disguised as a nightmare, problem or a waste of time. However, opportunity was there. In fact, opportunity is **always** present.

The co-worker's performance on the new assignment could have been the opportunity to work hard and impress the decision makers with his or her skills, thus earning a promotion. A date with an unpopular guy was an opportunity to have a new friend. Who knows? That "goofy" guy could have become more than a friend – he could have grown up to become Mr. Right with contacts for his eyes and a successful business. Speaking on behalf of the powerless was an opportunity to affect positive change in the lives of others. It was an opportunity to help someone. Nevertheless, the opportunity was missed!

Let me say again: *Opportunity is always present!*

I realize that saying opportunity is always present may not seem to make much sense. My life was forever changed on May 28, 2014. It will never be the same. I will never be the same. However, I believe in my heart that my personal loss is an opportunity for me to be better. Brooks passing away is bigger than him. It is bigger than me. In the flesh, it makes no sense that my children's father and hero are no longer here. I may not understand the purpose for such an unexpected and devastating blow to my family; however, what I do believe and understand is that God's grace is sufficient and ALL things work together for the good of those who love the Lord and are called for His purpose. This experience is an opportunity for God's glory to be manifested and His peace to give comfort to endure the days ahead.

So what do you do?

Being open to the idea that opportunity is always present is an excellent start. *It Ain't Over!* was written to encourage and offer the reader a strategy to increase the number of opportunities one will experience. In so doing, one can also experience a more fulfilling and successful life – personally and professionally. This book introduces the reader to four principles that, if implemented consistently, will result in countless opportunities. The concepts introduced are based on first-hand knowledge, experience, observations and the advice of mentors. Throughout this book, both real life examples and hypothetical scenarios are included to drive home the point **"It Ain't Over!"**

I often wondered how I was supposed to achieve success without first having an opportunity. There was a time I'd convinced myself external forces were hindering my success. It wasn't *my* fault opportunity wasn't knocking at my door. Eventually, however, I came to the realization that I had to take responsibility and look inwardly for both the cause of my problem and the solution.

I needed to do something different. Instead of viewing the situation as a problem, nightmare or waste of time, I needed to change my perspective. This so-called "problem" presented a perfect opportunity for me to come up with a solution to increase the number of opportunities that knocked at my door. Indeed, a solution did eventually emerge that changed my entire outlook on both opportunities and what it really means to be successful.

The solution to my "so-called" problem was the creation of a formula. When implemented consistently, each factor – reputation (R), resilience (R), relationships (R) and resurrection (R) – represents a principle contributing to the realization of opportunities (O).

$$O = R^3/R \text{ or } O = (R \times R \times R)/R$$

If math was not your favorite subject, don't worry. This is not as complicated as it may appear. It will become clear in the following pages.

The formula has been tried and tested. In fact, I've been sharing this formula with friends and those I've mentored for years. I have no doubt that had I *not* followed the principles, I would not be where I am today. I definitely would not have had the confidence to write a book about it.

For me, this formula resulted in much more than opportunities for success, experience and/or failure. Through this formula, I gained increased patience along with an attitude adjustment. My relationships became more valued and cherished. This formula helped me become a better person and live a more fulfilling life. My faith walk became stronger. And with each passing day, I came to appreciate the journey as I began living by the mantra: **"It Ain't Over!"**

So can you.

As you explore, it is my hope you will discover a new idea; affirm what you already know; and be encouraged to press on despite the circumstances. That is exactly what I was doing before May 28, 2014. That is what I continue to do after May 28, 2014.

PART I:

IT AIN'T OVER!

Before I go any further, I must set the record straight. I am well aware that the title of the book is grammatically incorrect. To all my English teachers who taught me the proper way to construct a sentence, I offer my deepest and sincerest apologies. My choice of wording bears no reflection upon your instruction. I made a conscious decision to select a title that was grammatically incorrect. I had absolutely no choice.

I always asked Brooks what he thought of a particular title. His response was usually "no, try again". The same was true when I pitched *It Is Not Over.* This title just did not have the same ring to my ears, nor his. It didn't sound *right* at all. I tried to make it work. I said it over and over and over again: "It is not over!" "It is not over!" "It is not over!". That sentence just could not convey the proper meaning of my true feelings. However, when I said **"It Ain't Over!"** with a touch of attitude and a boatload of confidence, I knew it was the right title for the right topic for the right reason – and so did Brooks.

The statement **"It Ain't Over!"** has served me well for many years. In times of challenge, self-doubt, despair and now a very, very, very horrible nightmare, I would encourage myself by saying: "It ain't over until I'm six feet under." The irony is not lost on me and, while some may consider this line of thinking as somewhat extreme or even morbid, I believe extreme circumstances call for extreme measures.

These three little words – **"It Ain't Over!"** – can change one's perspective, disposition and drive. They can change one's outlook on the future. There are countless examples of widely known events and personalities that demonstrate that it's never completely over. What seems bleak today can appear bright tomorrow. There is always an opportunity to make a comeback from a setback. A comeback from a setback is possible even under the most challenging circumstances. When you are out matched or have demonstrated bad judgment; when obstacles abound and indiscretions have occurred; when all hope is gone, knowing **"It Ain't Over"** reassures that achieving success is still within reach. To support my theory consider the following:

- Nobel Peace Prize Winner, Nelson Mandela
- Pro Golfer, Tiger Woods
- 2013 Iron Bowl Game, University of Alabama versus Auburn University
- American Idol Runner Up, Jennifer Hudson
- My Savior, Jesus Christ

You may be familiar with some of the names and events listed. In each case, no one would have imagined a comeback was possible. However, in each scenario, not only was there an opportunity to launch a comeback, but one that was bigger, better and achieved much success. While these were well-known personalities and events, the **same theory holds true for every person. Opportunity doesn't discriminate.** *I know this to be true more now than ever.*

Mrs. Malone's Rum Cake

I can personally attest to the value of believing and hoping there is always a chance for things to work out. When I was a child, we had a neighbor named Mrs. Malone. The décor of her home was classic grandma's house. Everything had a special place and each item was in its place. There were family photos, plastic flowers, tiny knickknacks on the coffee table and the smell of spicy/sweet perfume in the air. I would visit Mrs. Malone often and assist her with simple household chores such as cooking, reading her mail and writing out checks for her bills.

Watching Mrs. Malone was my first exposure to how opportunity is always present. I learned early that opportunity is more about your perception rather than your circumstances – Mrs. Malone was blind. She always looked so neat and nice. I found it amazing, the things she would do without having her sight. She went to church every Sunday. She cleaned and cooked. She made cakes during the holidays. (I especially enjoyed tasting the batter of her rum cake. Perhaps it had something to do with the rum.)

Mrs. Malone could have very easily accepted her physical challenge as an opportunity to be totally dependent. However, she did not allow her disability to hinder her from living a fulfilled life. Not having your sight can obviously be very limiting; yet, Mrs. Malone carried herself as if it wasn't. Clearly, she recognized the opportunity to live her life the best way she knew how. She took the opportunity to live without limits.

Where's Mr. Right?

Coming from a large family, I always imagined being a wife and mother. I dreamed of being happily married with children. I just knew I would be married once I finished college. However, that didn't happen. Then I knew I would get married by the time I was twenty-seven. That didn't happen. Then I knew I would get married by the time I was thirty. Well, *that* didn't happen either.

It seemed that everyone around me was having the opportunity to live my dream. There was wedding after wedding, birth after birth and throughout this time, I was dating. Was there an opportunity to live out my dream with one of these suitors? Yes? Maybe? Possibly? Ok, no way! As much as I desired to be married, I had enough common sense not to settle for Mr. Wrong.

At the burial of each relationship, I started to seriously wonder about the existence of Mr. Right. Would he ever show so we could ride off into the sunset and live happily ever after? On several occasions, I was tempted to forget my dream and stay single forever. I also considered becoming a single parent. I could have accepted the invitations to become someone's "garden tool" or side chick. But I didn't. Instead, I decided to believe **"It Ain't Over!"**

Several more years would pass before Mr. Right finally arrived and my dream was realized. Because I refused to give up or settle, God blessed me with the opportunity to marry my best friend, Ivor, who I fondly called "Brooks." Yet, who could have predicted I would have to revisit and amend my draft for this publication just a few weeks before the scheduled print date because Brooks was called to be with the Lord? However, this, too, is an opportunity. Yes, I am sad for my boys and me, but we can find peace in trusting that God doesn't make mistakes.

I thank God for the *opportunity* to be married to a wonderful man who I know loved God and his family. Experiencing the joy of being married to a man who can be described as a loving, kind, strong, funny, visionary leader, protector, provider and my best friend for 14 years is more than a blessing. Some people don't get 14 days.

> **Word of Encouragement:** It is understandable to become tempted and discouraged when you're waiting for your dreams to come true and your blessings to arrive. Don't lose hope. Our time is not *His* time: "And let us not be weary in doing well; for in due season we shall reap, if we faint not." *Galatians 6:9*

The Death Sentence

Prior to May 28, 2014, I thought the real test of the mantra "It Ain't Over!" occurred for me in September 2008. What started out as a routine annual check-up led to a series of tests resulting in a breast cancer diagnosis. Words cannot describe how I felt. To say I was scared is an understatement. After May 28, 2014, cancer has moved to the number two spot on the "Oh my goodness. Why me Lord? Really, is this really happening to me?" list.

The emotional roller coaster I experienced had me believing the diagnosis was a death sentence. On the outside, I put my best face forward. On the inside, I was having a pity party and playing the "what if" game. What if the treatment doesn't work? What if the cancer returns? What if I die? The first day of radiation treatment was a major turning point. On that day, I was reminded that I wasn't dead yet – that **"It Ain't Over"**.

During this uncertain time and for the remainder of the treatments, I reflected on my Christian teachings for encouragement:

Words of Encouragement:
- Be of good courage for God is with thee.
- No weapon formed against me shall prosper.
- In all thy ways acknowledge Him and He shall direct your path.
- I will lift up my eyes to the hills – from whence comes my help? My help comes from the Lord.
- God does not give us a spirit of fear.

Once again, I find myself reflecting on my Christian teachings. I thought cancer was a death sentence. I was wrong. Cancer cannot compare to the emotions and grief that occurs when you lose a loved one – especially when it is sudden.

I am so very thankful that I have achieved success and have been cancer free for five years. I will achieve success again. Actually, it has already been achieved, depending on your perspective or whom you ask.

Whether it is a disability, disappointment, an unfulfilled dream, cancer, the threat of death or actual death, never give up hope. When you are tempted to consider or accept that opportunity isn't knocking at your door, open your eyes, listen to your heart and know **"It Ain't Over!"**

Playing Pretend

We can learn a lot from children. They naturally live like **"It Ain't Over!"** Children approach things from the perspective that there is nothing to lose. They see the possibilities in everything. They are not limited by the fears of past experiences or disappointments. They rebound very quickly following failure or disappointment. They see the good in most things and find ways to make other things better.

Children may very well have life figured out. It's not until we become adults that we manage to over complicate, over analyze and often become over loaded on life's journey. Children, however, they take life one day at a time, welcoming every opportunity and celebrating small achievements.

When I was a child, my Grandfather pronounced my name as Josh – at least, that's what it sounded like to me. We had a very special relationship. I would tag along behind him at every opportunity. I was so attached to him, I actually wanted his last name. Thus, the birth of one of my many personalities came to life: Josh Stone.

Let's take a look into Josh Stones' world. Josh was a very happy little girl. She was adventurous, curious and a natural performer. Playing pretend was her favorite game. She would take the simplest observation and turn it into a mini production, documentary or drama.

She earned the title "parrot" from her grandfather because whatever she heard she would repeat. Regurgitating someone else's words was accompanied by a change in voice pitch, facial expression and mannerisms. Everyone was a convenient candidate for imitation and no one was exempt – including grandparents, parents, sisters, brothers, pastor, the lady next door, the lady in church who got happy every Sunday at the same time, the mailman, cashiers and the garbage man. Television personalities were also perfect targets: the weatherman, Penny on "Good Times" and Bob Barker from the "Price Is Right."

Josh uncovered an opportunity to fill the day with some fun and laughter. How could this child's game of pretend be considered an opportunity? That was the beauty of Josh's mind. An *adult* mind would quickly label this activity childish; however, Josh was actually developing an undercover opportunity with lasting beneficial outcomes.

To play this game Josh needed two things: a "target" and an audience. Once a target was identified, she sought out an audience. When an audience was not available to see the latest performance, she found opportunity in a mirror – with an audience of one and reflected laughter.

Mother would pass by and see Josh in the mirror pretending to be anyone and everyone – her antics quickly followed by the uninhibited laughter of an innocent child. Josh often moved the performances outside in the backyard by the fence where she had to set the stage. She'd turn the garbage can upside-down to serve as a podium and place a lawn chair behind the garbage can to serve as the pastor's chair. Then it was time to have a little church.

Josh would begin by saying: "Open your Bibles and turn to the second chapter of Exodus, read along as I read aloud … Amen. This morning I would like to talk to you on the subject, "Ain't No Time like the Present." In the backyard behind an overturned garbage can, she became a Southern Baptist minister with a Dixie cup of water to sip and a paper towel to wipe the sweat. Before long, friends would join the game of pretend and begin to imitate people they'd seen in church shouting and performing the holy dance.

It may seem childish, but this game of pretend offered much more than fun and laughter. Academic development and character-building benefits were the by-products. Josh's ability and skills to hear and recall were the same skills needed in the classroom. Her language skills were improved. She gained confidence, high self-esteem and a willingness to share – the same traits most employers look for in a new hire.

Josh carried those skills and abilities into adulthood. Pretending was much more than a childish game; it was an opportunity to grow into an articulate, confident, and giving adult.

Is that not success?

As we grow older, if we can hold on to the simple pleasures and possess a willingness to take a risk, we will discover or uncover opportunities. I'm not suggesting throwing all caution to the wind. I'm suggesting that there is something to gain from simply trying. Before we label an opportunity as trouble or a waste of time, we should seek to uncover and explore the possibilities.

One Man's Trash is Another Man's Treasure

Opportunities abound and success is in reach. However, you must first believe it to achieve it. An opportunity to one person does not necessarily appear as an opportunity to another. The same is true about success. Your perception will determine what is or isn't an opportunity and what is or isn't success.

Success or failure is often the result of one's perception, resilience, willingness to work and faith. No one hesitates to take credit for successful results. The opposite should also hold true.

If an opportunity ends in total disappointment or absolute failure, who's responsible? In some cases, external factors may have contributed to the results. However, if not all the responsibility lies with the individual, most of it does.

Perception is powerful. Imagine driving down the street and seeing old furniture that has been discarded on the side of the road. One person would pass and never give it a first glance, much less a second glance. This person considers the discarded furniture as nothing more than trash.

Now, consider another person driving by and viewing the same discarded furniture. She stops and begins to take a closer look. She inspects the furniture, loads it in the vehicle and considers it a treasure. Once she invests some sweat equity in restoring the furniture, a gold mine will be discovered. What one person perceived as trash, someone else perceived as an opportunity.

This is a classic example of the power of perception. Whatever is perceived to be true is true. The first driver perceived the furniture as trash; therefore, it was trash. The second driver perceived the furniture as treasure and discovered a golden opportunity.

I speak of furniture, but the same is true in life. If you perceive something to be bad, it's bad. That's the way you will approach, think and respond to it. However, if you perceive something to be good, it's good. Again, that's the way you will approach, think and respond to it.

Consider these examples and ask yourself: Is it over or is it an opportunity?

Example: Imagine a young lady who dreamed of marrying her high school sweet heart and living happily ever after. To her disappointment and heartbreak, the relationship imploded. Where is the opportunity in this situation? How could this possibly be an opportunity?

This young lady now has the chance (opportunity) to determine the next step that should be taken. Because of her broken heart, she has the option to mistrust every man she meets in the future, resulting in a series of up and down relationships, never lasting long and probably ending on bad a note. However, there is also the *opportunity* to learn from the situation and look forward to a new and better relationship in the future. It all boils down to how she perceives and defines the situation. Is it over? Or is it an opportunity?

Example: The school your child attends has a reputation of not having the best curriculum, instructors or facilities. Your child is not failing; however, you hope for better circumstances. You value education and have higher expectations, but removing your child from the school is not an option at this time.

There are other options (opportunities) to consider:
- Partner with your child's teacher to ensure his education is not compromised.

- Introduce other activities to supplement his education such as camps, clubs and after school programs.

- Join the PTA and work from the inside to improve the circumstances.

- Evaluate your finances, tighten your belt and make the sacrifices necessary to transfer your child to a different school.

- Surrender that this is the way it is going to be and hope for the best.

Your perception of the situation will dictate how you will respond and directly influence the outcomes. Is it over? Or is it an opportunity?

The take-away in the previous examples are very simple: *You hold the key – not only to your opportunity, but to the success or failure as well.*

The principles introduced throughout this book will serve as a reminder of the power you possess in charting your own course, increasing your opportunities and creating your own success – allowing three little words to lead to a fulfilling life, both personally and professionally.

NOTES

PART II:

THE FORMULA

No GPS on the Road to Success

The road to success is often filled with turns, twists, roadblocks and detours. If one could have a GPS system on this journey, a lot of heartache, headaches, disappointments and setbacks could be avoided. Unfortunately, life does not come with instructions, maps or navigation systems. The best we can do is identify a destination and then do the work required to get there – which is sometimes easier said than done.

Success varies based on perception. Regardless of how you define success, one thing is for sure: More often than not, the road to success can be found at the intersection of opportunity and hard work. The more opportunities that come your way, the more chances there are to experience success as long as you are willing to do the work – the actions necessary to position one for success.

If it seems like a long time since you heard opportunity knock at your door, don't be discouraged. **"It Ain't Over!"** Consider digging deeper to discover that opportunity ... or listen a little closer to hear the knock. With that in mind, the first order of business is to ensure opportunity comes your way.

The Formula. The goal of the formula is to introduce four key principles that, when implemented, will assist in realizing opportunities and, ultimately, success. The formula did not evolve over night. It developed over two decades as I learned lessons from my own experiences and observations and listened to the advice of mentors. Each factor individually is an important principle to follow; however, when the factors are placed in the same formula, it equates to opportunity.

$$O = R^3/R \text{ or } O = (R \times R \times R) / R$$

O = opportunity, R = reputation, R = resilience,
R = relationships and R = resurrection. So now you have:

**Opportunity = <u>Reputation x Resilience x Relationships</u>
Resurrection**

Let's explore each factor individually.

Opportunity = Reputation

Character Counts

People who are successful are usually known for having a good or (even better) an excellent reputation. Having this type of reputation tends to invite opportunity. Reputation is how others perceive, think or form opinions about your values, morals, integrity and character. Educational background, experience, associations, attitude, work ethic and treatment of others are also attributes that add to the assessment of one's reputation.

There are all types of reputations. Everyone has one. A reputation can be described as excellent, good, bad, suspect, questionable – or with more colorful language we'll leave for another discussion. One thing is for certain: no one in the world wants to offer you an opportunity if you don't, at the very least, possess a good reputation.

Character is very likely one of the most important elements when it comes to reputation. Character speaks of your moral and ethical qualities. I define character as the way one thinks, feels and behaves. It has been said time and time again that *character counts*. Without character, what kind of opinions will be formed about you? How will it affect your reputation? How will it affect your opportunities? More importantly, how will it affect your success?

For comparison sake, let's look at a person who has a bad reputation. This individual may be described as one that cannot be trusted – a slacker, an arrogant, self-absorbed opportunist (as well as a few adjectives I choose not to write – although you know what they are). Clearly, an individual known for these traits should not be surprised if no one knocks at his door. Having a bad reputation is an obstacle to being considered for an opportunity. A bad reputation can hinder the chances to success.

Guarding Your Reputation

You must guard your reputation at all times. Reputation is like glass. Once it's broken, it's very difficult to put back together. It takes many years to build a good reputation but only a few seconds to tear it down. If you lose the designation of a "good reputation", an enormous amount of time and energy is necessary to reclaim and restore it. Therefore, it's best to use the time and energy to build, protect and maintain your good reputation. Again, you must ***guard and protect*** the reputation at all times. After all, anything that takes a lifetime to build and seconds to destroy deserves your complete attention.

Words, deeds and associations are the most common factors that can positively or negatively affect a reputation in. What do you say? What do you do? With whom do you associate? Your response to each question is critical to your reputation. There are many examples of individuals who had excellent reputations and then one act of bad behavior resulted in the loss of opportunities, careers, endorsements, position, spouses, financial stability and even their freedom. I need not call their names; they are not difficult to find. Look to the government, sports, military, music industry and even the pulpit for a short list.

It may not seem fair for a person to work long and hard to build a reputation and then, in the blink of the eye, damage it or lose it completely over one thing. However, there is always a bright side. Once the reputation is lost or damaged, it can be regained. **"It Ain't Over!"** Although it will require unwavering determination, commitment and hard work to restore it.

> **A word of advice:** It is easier to guard and protect your reputation than to lose it and have to rebuild it.

Do you recall this old saying: "Birds of the same feather flock together."? It's an example of how easy it is to affect your reputation. If you are seen frequently associating with individuals with questionable reputations, it will not be long before others will assume your reputation is questionable as well. Whether true or not, people often form their opinions based on perception. Or, I should probably say, people form opinions about your reputation on what they *think* they see. However, the reverse also applies.

If you are seen frequently associating with individuals who are respected and held in high regard, it will not be long before you are regarded in the same light. "Birds of the same feather flock together."

Your reputation is what people say about you when you are not present. In the case of business, when your name comes up in a discussion and you are not present, the responses should include positive statements: Hard worker, dependable, a real team player, always willing to help, I would love to have him/her on my team. It is cause for concern that if, in your absence, your name comes up and no one has anything good to say – or they choose to say nothing at all.

Assessing Your Reputation

What's your reputation? First and foremost, it is not always what you think. Your reputation is defined by what other people think or perceive about you. I suggest you identify three people you trust – individuals you know will always tell you the truth. These three people you should be diverse to ensure you receive different perspectives. I frequently call upon one of my six siblings. They have absolutely no problem telling me about myself. I also call upon a long-time mentor, Reginald Murchison, because I know, without doubt, his feedback will be brutal but honest. He has helped guide my view on the importance of a good reputation and often says: "You live and die by your reputation." Lastly, I would seek the input of my husband. He served as a mirror for me and would tell me exactly what he sees. This process has served me well through the years.

Academy Award Winning Performance

I was once given what I consider a comprehensive professional assessment that would indicate strengths, weaknesses, where improvement was needed, risk for workplace violence and so forth. The results of my assessment said I could be intimidating and overly excitable. My initial response was very defensive because I did not want to believe this to be true. I felt it was a negative, slanderous, total misrepresentation of my character. Turns out ... well, not necessarily. I sought out several trusted, independent critics and, to my surprise, they had the same assessment. They saw the same thing. It was true!

I confess I can often be direct. Unfortunately, my ability to be direct was perceived as being intimidating. Secondly, I *am* excitable. I do talk with my hands and can be animated. At times, I can even be a little dramatic – Academy Award winning dramatic.

Knowledge is powerful. Knowing where this was coming from, I had a choice in the matter. I could continue to be the same and be prepared to accept whatever the consequences were *or* I could alter my behavior to ensure my reputation was not being adversely affected by the way others perceived me. I decided to do the latter. Knowing what the issue was, I took steps to dispel the misconceptions. Since my direct statements caused others to feel intimidated, I simply would rephrase my statements in a way that would make the point – in a less pointed manner. Knowing that my animation tended to appear overly excitable, I was more conscious and toned it down. Prior to seeking the feedback of others, I never had a clue that those behaviors were an issue. It could have been the cause for opportunity to *not* knock at my door.

If you are not sure of your reputation, it doesn't cost you anything to seek out unbiased assessors. Once you receive the assessment, the ball is in your court. What you do from that point is up to you. You have the opportunity and the power to respond as desired.

You Be the Judge

As stated earlier, words, deeds and associations are the most common factors that can affect a reputation in a positive or negative manner. What you say, what you do and who you associate with affect your reputation. Building your reputation is not a one-time activity. Your reputation is built daily and refined over time. How you carry yourself, choice of wardrobe, the words that come out of your mouth and how you react to adversity are a few of the various factors that contribute to your reputation. Remember: reputation is how others interpret your character and qualities.

In the following examples, you be the judge:

Example 1: Stilettos

Imagine that a certain person was applying for a position as a stocker in a warehouse. When she arrived for the interview, she was 15 minutes late and offered no apology or explanation. Her attire included a very short skirt, tight revealing blouse, stiletto heels and very long, colorful acrylic nails. During the interview, her cell phone rang and she looked at it to see who was calling. What company or business will hire individuals who appear rude, tardy and obviously unaware of the job requirements for a stocker in a warehouse? Who wears stilettos to this type of interview? What sort of reputation do you think she was perceived to have? Would you hire her?

Example 2: Cover Blown on the 16ᵗʰ Hole

There is a time and place for everything – and it is good to know the environment, culture and expectations. As the saying goes: "When it Rome, do as the Romans". I recall one of the first times I played in a charity golf tournament. Although I had the clubs, bag, shoes, gloves and golf apparel, I was not familiar with the rules of the game. However, I looked like I was. I wanted to be perceived as an experienced golfer. I managed to conceal my inexperience pretty well. I wasn't Tiger Woods, but I was holding my own. I made it to the 15ᵗʰ hole and imagined my teammates thought I was a decent golfer and a good sport up to that point.

The reputation I had built through 15 rounds of golf was blown on the 16ᵗʰ hole. It was my turn to putt after my three teammates missed their putts. The pressure was building. Everyone was depending on me so we could make par. Golf is considered a gentleman's game. If one does well, you shake hands or say "Good shot fellow." Not me! I made the putt. We made par. I was so excited I totally forgot where I was and an Academy Award winning performance ensued. I immediately jumped up and starting doing a happy dance while chanting: "Go Joyce E, Go Joyce E., Go....." When I stopped, I could tell by the expressions on my teammates' faces I had managed to blow my reputation – but I made the putt!

I share this as a simple and somewhat embarrassing example of how hard it is to build your reputation and how quickly it can be torn down. Seriously, it doesn't take a lot to damage your reputation. Having a good reputation tends to invite opportunity to your door. Don't let a lapse in judgment, a slip of the tongue or suspect associations affect your reputation. Remember, character counts!

Nothing nor anyone is perfect. Therefore, I will not mislead you into thinking you must have a perfect reputation. Having one that you can be proud of is good enough. **Of course, having a reputation your mother will be proud of is even better.**

Opportunity = Reputation x Resilience

Stay in the Game

The next factor in the formula is Resilience (R). Resilience is the capacity to recover quickly from difficulties and unforeseen challenges. Imagine that you really wanted to have the opportunity to experience a long desired dream – perhaps the chance to travel abroad for your company or hear wedding bells after meeting Mr. Right. Or maybe you were expecting a raise or promotion. But your dream didn't happen. You didn't hear wedding bells. (It was probably a siren warning you of Mr. Wrong.) Or maybe a memo circulates that all raises, promotions and company travel are frozen until further notice.

The common examples listed above could cause a person to become frustrated and just want to give up. However, being resilient enables you to man up (or woman up) and endure mental, physical or emotional hardship and disappointment. **Being resilient encourages you to accept the circumstances, remain optimistic, expect other opportunities to come your way and stay in the game.**

Easier said than done, I know. However, combining your good reputation with the ability to be resilient is a formula for opportunity to come knocking at your door.

Remember: At the intersection of opportunity and hard work is where you will surely find success.

The Waiting Game

Now that you have built a good reputation and you are guarding your reputation closely, the waiting game begins. It can seem like forever when you are waiting for an opportunity to come your way. However, be encouraged. Not only will opportunities come your way, there is the possibility opportunity has already knocked. It may very well be another case of an opportunity disguised as a problem or a nightmare. A wise person can see past the problem and identify the possibilities. So before you say "I never get a break; opportunity never knocks at my door; I give up" – hold on! **"It Ain't Over!"**

"Inside of every problem lies an opportunity."
~ Robert Kiyosaki,
Author of *Rich Dad, Poor Dad*

Consider a football or basketball player who has been practicing and preparing all season for the game. He has on his uniform, knows the plays and is mentally and physically ready to contribute to the success of the team. Yet, for whatever reason, there he sits, on the bench, waiting for the coach to call his name.

Preparation is key. When opportunity finally arrives, the last thing you want is not to be ready. Fortunately, the player was ready had he been called. Unfortunately, the player was left wondering what would have happened if he'd been given the opportunity to play. Is he really on the team or is he a bench warmer? He must be resilient enough to not become dismayed and throw in the towel.

<u>Maybe it is time to perform an assessment.</u>

This assessment is more about looking inward than outward. What must I do to get in the game? Have I dotted my I's and crossed my T's? Is my reputation as good as I think it is? Should I take this time as an opportunity to sharpen my skills, learn a new skill, go back to school or volunteer to expand my experiences? There are more questions to ask. But the point is clear: a resilient person will view the waiting game as an opportunity to prepare for when the door opens. A resilient person will use this "down time" to better themselves, become more productive and gain some patience.

> "I will prepare and some day my chance will come."
> ~ Abraham Lincoln

Have you ever heard the cliché a watched pot never boils? Nothing ever seems to happen when you expect it to happen. I have no doubt it will happen, but you have to stay in the game to realize it. That's what having resilience will enable you to do. Everyone experiences the highs and lows of life.

What distinguishes the winners from losers is their commitment to press on in spite of the delays, disappointments or detours. Winners stay in the game! Winners understand that **"It Ain't Over!"**

What Not to Do

It has been said that confession is good for the soul but bad for the reputation. I have a slightly different take. When confession becomes an opportunity to encourage someone or help one avoid making a mistake, then confession is very good and worth the risk. The objective is to increase your opportunities, not to decrease them.

What I'm about to share is an example in what not to do, especially if you're working to increase your opportunities. Resilience would have been a very helpful trait to possess in this case. Unfortunately, my resilience was on vacation.

It was Friday. I had been in a meeting that afternoon and placed my cell phone on silent. When the meeting was over, I forgot to take it off the silent setting. I left the office around five and headed home for a welcomed weekend. That night when I took my phone out of my purse, I realized I had several missed calls from the same person. Since it was after 10 p.m., I decided I would wait till morning to return the call.

I returned the call first thing Saturday morning only to be greeted with what I sensed as anger followed by instructions to appear in their office first thing Monday morning. You can only imagine how I felt for the next 48 hours. I took it personally and was very concerned about what to expect on Monday morning. Considering I prided myself on my reputation, I knew this wasn't going to be good.

On Monday morning, I arrived bright and early prepared for some mentoring, coaching or counseling. I walked into the department head's office, said good morning and moved to take a seat, but was instructed to remain standing because the meeting would not take long. And it didn't. I was told in no uncertain terms that my failure to respond to the cell phone call in a timely manner was not a good reflection on the position I held and it was not to happen again! Yes, that is what was said. Wow!!

This was clearly a lesson in what not to do. If the roles had been switched, I would have *never* been that direct or cold. However, I confess, my response wasn't much better. For the next five days, I intentionally avoided any communications or interactions. Resilience was still on vacation. I did not bounce back well. I would have personally benefitted greatly if I'd just possessed a little resilience. Instead, I acted like a child, a spoiled brat. I lost seven days of joy by focusing on this one mistake. On that Friday, we talked again about the incident and came to a respectful understanding.

The reality is no one is perfect. The test of true character is how you respond in the face of adversity. I confess I failed miserably in this example because I couldn't see the opportunities that existed in this circumstance. Looking at the situation in the rear view mirror, I can now see there were several opportunities for me to show resilience, demonstrate maturity and effectively communicate. My greatest take-away was I learned **"What Not to Do!"**

Not About Me

Just because something does or doesn't happen as you would expect doesn't always mean it's about you – nor should you make it about you. I challenge you to focus on the needs of others. While you are waiting, you can help someone prepare or receive his/her next opportunity. ***"Do unto others as you would have them do unto you"***. I believe when you bless others, you are blessed in turn. Some may describe these acts as karma. Call it what you like. What comes around goes around. Or vice versa – what goes around comes around.

Bored and Homesick

When I first moved to Birmingham following college to accept a new job, I didn't know anyone and found myself homesick. I went to work and came home to an empty apartment. I found myself questioning my decision to move to a City where I had neither family nor friends. I eventually surrendered and decided to make the best of the situation.

Once I stopped spending my time having pity parties and started volunteering and helping others, things got better. I used this time as an opportunity to share my time, gifts and talents. I tutored. I wrote plays for the youth department at 16th Street Baptist Church. I joined a few professional organizations. It wasn't long before I had more friends and more things to do. Because I saw an opportunity to do something productive with this extra time on my hand, I received what I was missing. Resilience helped me to stay in the game and not pack my bags and head home to LA (Lower Alabama).

Friendly Warning

Resilience is an excellent character trait to possess. Resilience is a compliment to your reputation. However, if you're not a resilient person, be prepared for some unexpected consequences such as stress, frustration, poor attitude, hopelessness, suspicions and so forth. Don't believe me? Think about your family, inner circle or anyone who has been on the same team or project with you.

When they are required to wait or things aren't happening on their time line, what emotions or behaviors have been observed? Stress? Frustration? Attitude? Anger? All of the above?

Impatience could result in turning to vices or behaviors that are not healthy. A vice isn't always drugs, alcohol or questionable behavior. A vice is anything you seek to soothe the disappointments on the road to success. I, too, had my share of vices, including sweet binges, shopping until I dropped, bad relationships, playing the victim and drinking too much sweet tea. Yes, sweet tea. (I am Southern, after all.) These behaviors resulted in nothing more than me feeling fat, broke, lonely and depressed. I am very thankful those days are behind me! Believe in yourself and open your eyes to the possibilities.

Before you throw in the towel and give up, step back, exhale, and create your own opportunities while you wait. Whatever you do: **"Stay in the Game!"**

Opportunity = Reputation x Resilience x Relationships

Building A Network: 360° Relationships

Let's explore the third factor in the equation: relationships. Relationships are the way in which people connect or behave toward one another. Before you can establish healthy, productive associations with others, there are two very important relationships that should be cultivated and maintained.

A Relationship with God

I believe the first and most important relationship should be with God. I understand that spirituality has varying interpretations so this principle is inclusive of all faiths and whomever you choose to honor or worship. If you choose not to have a belief in a higher power, that's an individual choice and I will be the first not to judge. As for me and my house, we will serve the Lord.

With that said, I choose to have a relationship with Jesus Christ. As a result, I know without a doubt that I am loved unconditionally and I am never alone. In every relationship, there is give and take. I have been given much more than I will ever be able to repay. I am so appreciative to live in a country where we all have the opportunity to worship and serve whomever we choose without fear.

Sometimes when it feels like nothing is going my way, I turn to a power much greater than myself. Life is unpredictable. Did I not just say a mouth full? Today, you have a job. Tomorrow you are laid off. Today, you are in a happy marriage or partnership, tomorrow you don't know this person anymore or he is gone to Glory. One thing I know for sure: whether it is yesterday, today or tomorrow, God is the same. Through my own eyes, I often see failure, inadequacy, weakness and imperfections. Through His eyes, He sees the best in me. In times when I can neither see nor hear opportunity – when I think things are over – my relationship with God assures me that: **"It Ain't Over!"**

Whomever you choose to call your God, I encourage you to treat this relationship with the highest respect and honor. A loving relationship with God makes all other relationships a lot easier to establish and maintain. If you have not chosen to seek a relationship with God, I respectfully invite you to get to know mine. He has never failed nor forsaken me. He will do the same for you.

A Relationship with Self

The second most important relationship is the one you have with yourself. It's very simple: love yourself. The ability to love yourself is imperative for a healthy self-image and self-respect. The way you connect or behave toward another is a reflection of how you feel about yourself. Sometimes we can be our own worst critics. Yes, you should hold yourself to a higher standard. However, if you fail to reach it, forgive yourself and try again. **"It Ain't Over!"** Believe in yourself. No one is perfect and we all make mistakes. See the opportunities that exist by just being "the best you" you can be.

When a person possesses a negative image, low self-esteem, bad attitude, anger or a sense of hopelessness, they bring that into their relationships. Think about domestic violence, child abuse, hate crimes and crimes against another person. Individuals who inflict these heinous acts do not have any love or respect for themselves. These are extreme examples, but the principle is the same. A person cannot give what they do not have. How is one expected to be respectful if they do not have self-respect?

Activity: Think about what you see when you look in the mirror. Were your thoughts positive or negative? I hope positive. Now, let's be intentional and commit to only positive thoughts about yourself. Complete the following sentence, ten times:

I am_____.

Example: I am a beautiful inside and out. I am dependable. I am deserving.

Continue to practice this exercise daily until your positive thoughts flow without pausing. It should become very easy to think well of yourself.

Building Relationships

Although it should have been pretty obvious how important it is to establish and cultivate relationships, I confess the importance of relationships didn't occur to me until I was well into my career. I mentioned earlier how my parents raised my siblings and me to have a good reputation and get a good education. Relationships were not at the top of their list. Actually, my father discouraged me from having too many relationships. He always warned about trusting too many people. Without question, I followed suit. My circle of friends was quite small.

It seemed normal to focus my energy on building a good reputation, working hard and not focusing on relationships. Now, however, I understand my energy should be on all three: reputation, hard work and relationships. ***Building relationships is <u>essential</u> to increasing your opportunities.*** The relationships you establish today may help open a door tomorrow.

When the Benefit of the Doubt Wasn't an Option

I recall at one point during my career a specific meeting of department heads and office managers to identify individuals who would be given the opportunity for additional training and exposure by transferring them to different locations in the region. As names were introduced, the managers discussed each candidate's experience, reputation and potential for advancement. How do I know this? Relationships. The discussion and what was said when my name was introduced was shared with me by one of the attendees. There was one person who really did not know me but based my reputation on the rumor mill – on information that was not good or accurate. The person clearly did not give me the benefit of the doubt. This is a perfect example of how fragile a reputation can be – and how important it is to guard it.

Fortunately, I had solid relationships with others participants in the meeting who were able to speak on my behalf and dispel many of the inaccuracies that were said about me. However, it was not enough to overcome what had already been said. Therefore, should be no surprise that I was not offered an opportunity.

Resilience was needed during this time as I continued to build and rebuild my reputation.

Realistically, there is no way to avoid people talking about you. Whether you are doing well or struggling, someone will eventually have something negative to say. Haters do exist. Everyone is not happy for your success. Maybe they are jealous. Maybe they heard something through the grapevine. Maybe they are projecting their personal issues with you. Maybe they just don't like you. In the grand scheme, however, none of these things matter. What does matter is that you remain resilient in the face of adversity and continue to love yourself.

360° Relationships – Building a Network

The type of relationships that are crucial are 360° Relationships. It seems natural to establish relationships with people you perceive have power or influence such as your supervisor. This approach, however, is extremely narrow. Yes, you should have a relationship with upper management and/or the person you report to, but you should never discount anyone. 360° Relationships include those you consider as your peers, those who support you and those you support. Family, work, church and community are *all* places where relationships should be cultivated.

Mr. Allen and Mr. Holmes: Divine Providence

While in college, I worked at the paper mill as an electrical engineer cooperative education student (co-op). There I began practicing the art of 360° Relationships, although I didn't know it at the time. A benefit of being a co-op student is the opportunity to gain real-life experience before graduating. The experience gained gives one a competitive advantage when applying for jobs following graduation.

I established relationships with the engineers in the department, my manager, managers in other departments, administrative assistants, the electricians in the plant, the ladies in the cafeteria, the HR director, security and so forth. When establishing these relationships, I had no idea I was creating a network – I was just excited to have a job, and I loved talking to everyone. I mean everyone. 360° Relationships are a solid start to building a network.

Establishing a network offers the opportunity to connect or link with individuals who can influence and offer benefits through a relationship. In choosing people for your network, look for those with integrity, a willingness to share their knowledge, mutual respect and, last but not least, someone you trust. If the individual does not meet the criteria, then they are classified as an acquaintance.

There was a very nice electrician in the plant by the name of Mr. Oliver Allen. We would frequently talk about school, careers, life and other topics of importance. He was a mentor to me. Mr. Allen would always tell me: "When you get ready to graduate and start looking for a job, let me know." He had a close relative who was high up in the electric utility. Because of my relationship with Mr. Allen, he introduced me to Mr. Robert Holmes.

When I met with Mr. Holmes at his office, he talked about careers at the company, why it would be a great company to work for and advised me on what I should do to increase my chances for employment. Well, I listened, did as I was instructed and, following graduation, I began my career with Alabama Power. But that's not the end of the story.

I never imagined that meeting Mr. Allen would have such a profound effect on my career. Mr. Allen was my mentor in the plant. Then, Mr. Holmes became a mentor, friend and someone who continues to advise me. More than two decades after our first encounters, we are all still connected. I have truly been the benefactor of these relationships. I know this had to be divine intervention because there is no way I can take credit for connecting the relationship dots so perfectly.

Mr. Holmes gave me advice that has served me well over the years. My connection to Mr. Holmes only came about because I had a relationship with Mr. Oliver. If I had excluded people from my network who didn't hold high positions or have a big title, I would have missed the opportunity to have lasting relationships and to learn major lessons from Mr. Holmes that have guided me through my entire career.

"It is better to be prepared for an opportunity when it presents itself than to have an opportunity presented and not be prepared." ~ Robert Holmes

In my previous example, the relationship timeline has lasted more than twenty years. I have also experienced the same benefits from a network where the timeline was much shorter. Within a 12-month period, I went from being a guest speaker for a college to a guest speaker for a national conference to a guest speaker for a state-wide association. This was all due to relationships.

I was asked to present a program based on my first book, *Self-Inflicted Overload* to graduate students at the University of Alabama at Birmingham. Following the speech, I spoke with the professor, Dr. Elizabeth Maples, who expressed her appreciation for the presentation. Not knowing at the time, this conversation was the beginning of a new relationship and future opportunities. Months later, I was invited to travel to Orlando, Florida by Dr. Maples to present the presentation again at a national conference. This was an excellent opportunity for exposure and building my network.

A few more months passed and I met with the professor and one of her colleagues to talk about hosting a program for business leaders. A few days later I received a call to speak at the Alabama Council of Association Executives' (ACAE) Winter Workshop. The organizer of the event told me the Greater Birmingham Convention and Visitors Bureau (CVB) referred me as a speaker. I contacted the person at the CVB to thank her for the referral. She said I should thank her contact at UAB, Paulisha Holt, who recommended me. To my surprise, her contact was Dr. Maples' colleague. This is not only an example of how relationships have an influence on opportunities, but it also demonstrates that networks do work.

But it doesn't end there! A person from another state-wide association attended ACAE's Winter Workshop and recommended me as the keynote speaker to nearly 550 people at the closing general session of her organization's annual convention. From that relationship, even more doors opened – further proof that the value of 360° Relationships is limitless.

Relationship vs. Acquaintance

I cannot express it enough that relationships are crucial. However, one would be wise to distinguish between a relationship and an acquaintance. At first glance, the two look and feel very similar because they both have a level of comfort in communicating, sharing and collaborating. There is a difference, however. Interactions through a *relationship* can lead to countless opportunities. On the other hand, treating an acquaintance in the same manner as a relationship carries more risk.

I can recall confiding and sharing my dreams and aspirations with people I believed to be friends and with whom I had good relationships. Unfortunately for me, they did not see our relationship in the same way. I was too trusting and obviously naïve. It never crossed my mind that someone would befriend me with the sole purpose to undermine me; yet, that's exactly what happened. Learning this lesson before it caused major turmoil or disappointment was an opportunity for me to distinguish between a true relationship and an acquaintance. Now I understand when my mother would say: **"Some people you need to feed with a long handled spoon."**

What I experienced is not new. It happens daily in business, families, congregations, government, the playground and anywhere people gather. Where you find people, you find individuals who may not be who they present themselves to be. It is your responsibility to be able to distinguish and discern what is true and what is not. As a member of a biker club would say: **"We ride till we die."** This is an example of a true relationship. It is easy to find individuals willing to ride. Finding individuals willing to die is a different story.

Friendly Reminder

Building relationships is <u>essential</u> to increasing your opportunities. As stated before, the two most important relationships are the ones established with God and self. Next, it is wise to include **360° Relationships** in your network. The criteria for including people in your network are: integrity, a willingness to share knowledge, mutual respect and trustworthiness. This should not be taken lightly. Individuals who do not meet the criteria are acquaintances. Proceed carefully and protect yourself from learning this lesson the hard way.

Opportunity = <u>Reputation x Resilience x Relationships</u>
Resurrection

Resurrection: It's Never Over

The last and most important factor in the formula is Resurrection. Resurrection is the foundation that undergirds all the factors. It is the ultimate validation of the premise of this book, ***It Ain't Over!***

Resurrection can be viewed as having three phases: initial, present and final. One may feel hopeless, threatened, forgotten and/or abandoned in phase one, the initial phase. From what appears to be an already bleak situation, we move to phase two, the present state. In the present state are the assessments, criticisms, and predictions for failure and doubts for the future. The third and final phase brings about revival, restoration, rebirth and RESURRECTION.

What do Mandela, Tiger, Jennifer, Auburn University and Ivor J. Brooks have in common?

Nelson Mandela was sentenced to five years in prison for inciting workers' strikes and leaving the country without permission. Later, Mr. Mandela and his comrades were charged with four counts of sabotage and conspiracy to overthrow the government. They were found guilty by South Africa's government and sentenced to life in prison for their offenses. Actually, Mandela was guilty of desiring and passionately calling for a color-blind South Africa. He remained in prison 27 years.

On February 11, 1990, hours after his release from prison Mandela vowed to end apartheid once and for all. Four years after his release from prison, he was elected President of the African National Congress. When he was incarcerated in 1964, few would have imagined Mandela would walk out of prison with even more passion for fighting for justice – not to mention becoming President. His body may have been imprisoned, but not his mind or spirit. He was resurrected to do great things following one of the greatest travesties of justice.

Tiger Woods is known as one of the best golfers in the world. In 2014, he had 79 official PGA events Masters, 14 majors and has broken countless records. In 2009, Mr. Woods became a media lightening rod following a public domestic incident between him and his wife. Every news outlet covered the story. Later, adding fuel to the tabloid frenzy, he had to deal with his high-profile divorce.

Following these events, it seemed as if Mr. Woods was struggling and could not return to the Championship status he once enjoyed. However, a resurrection was in the making. In

2013, he returned to the No. 1 spot in the world and his career was back on track.

In 2013, the University of Alabama played against Auburn University in the Iron Bowl. During the final moments of fourth quarter, with the score tied, Alabama attempted to kick a field goal. What happened next was nothing short of a rebirth for Auburn University. With 5 seconds left on the clock, the field goal fell short and Auburn cornerback Chris Davis caught the ball to run it back for a touchdown. Auburn University won the 2013 Iron Bowl game with only 5 seconds left on the clock and history was made.

Jennifer Hudson was an American Idol contestant during the show's third season. Simon Cowell, one of the show's judges, was very critical of the singer during the competition and she was voted off after he told her: "You're out of your depth in this competition."

Although Jennifer did not win (she actually finished seventh), she left the competition and went on to do great things, including winning both an Oscar and a Grammy as well as securing a role as the spokeswoman for Weight Watchers. She came back and came back big. Once again, someone who was counted out, experienced a resurrection.

I could site many more examples of resurrections, such as Helen Keller, Bill Clinton, Muhammad Ali, Diana Nyad, Wilma Rudolph, the Little Rock Nine and on and on to demonstrate that there is always an opportunity. In the face of trials, tragedy, criticism, age, doubt, obstacles, embarrassment, great odds and injustices there is an opportunity to be resurrected.

When I think about my husband, **Ivor J. Brooks**, I can't help but think how tragic it was for him to lose his life at the young age of 57, how he had so much more to experience – the milestones in his children and granddaughter's lives; the opportunity to affect positive changes for the fire service at the state and national levels; and, selfishly, to grow old with me. It's heartbreaking these things will never happen. Brooks is gone. The truth, however, is it is **NOT OVER** for Brooks. When you give your life to Christ, confess with your mouth and believe in your heart that He died for your sins, you are promised to live eternally with the King.

"For God so loved the world, that he gave his only begotten Son, that whosoever believeth in him should not perish but have everlasting life."
~ John 3:16

I know without doubt Brooks loved the Lord and gave Him his life. I find peace in knowing, although his earthly body has passed on, Brooks' spirit lives on. **It Ain't Over!** God is good and His word is true.

The greatest resurrection known worldwide is that of my Savior, Jesus Christ. Jesus made the ultimate sacrifice to save humanity. He represents all that is good and perfect. His reputation is unmatched and will never be diminished. Jesus was resilient, never giving up. He welcomed, established and continues to establish relationships with all people regardless of their sinful ways. As he ministered bringing love to a sinful world, he faced all kinds of challenges. He was criticized, betrayed, falsely accused and crucified. There is much more to tell of Jesus. However for brevity's sake, I will fast forward. His body was buried in a tomb guarded by soldiers. Three days following his death, when the ladies returned to the tomb, Jesus was not there. He had risen from the dead. He was resurrected!!

When they crucified the Savior, his accusers knew it was over. How wrong they were. It wasn't over then and **"It Ain't Over, now!"** He's coming back again.

The above examples prove once again, **"It Ain't Over!"** Opportunities are always present. It is your choice to believe this to be true. Life will always throw a curve ball, and you may even strike out from time to time. However, resurrection is as real as the nose on your face. Half of the battle to make a comeback and seize an opportunity is to believe it is possible. Maybe you just need to have a little faith. Faith is a powerful trait to possess.

> "Now faith is the substance of things hoped for, the evidence of things not seen." ~ Hebrews 11:1

Reputation, resilience and relationships individually can influence the arrival of an opportunity and, with hard work, there is a chance for success. There is a chance one will experience a fulfillment that offers peace in times of trouble. Hope in times of tragedy. Live in times of abandonment. However, when reputation, resilience and relationships are collectively undergirded by resurrection, the probability of success is greatly – sometimes amazingly – increased. In addition to opportunities, it also welcomes a feeling of fulfillment both personally and professionally.

PART III:

NO EXCUSES

It is easy to allow yourself to make excuses about how and why an opportunity was missed or failed to produce success. Excuses are nothing more than a lie dressed up. The best way to discourage the use of excuses is to expose how utterly ridiculous it is to attempt to hold others responsible for your failure to succeed.

The Indictment of "Mr. Opportunity"

As I look back over my life, I can recall categorizing opportunities when things did not go my way. I would think opportunity wasn't knocking or that I had completely missed an opportunity. I would then feel victimized by opportunity. In so doing, I adversely affected myself. I managed to perceive that my shortcomings, disappointments and failures were due to Mr. Opportunity.

There was a time I thought opportunity was more than a chance to try. Opportunity went beyond a word that is defined as a favorable or advantageous circumstance. I had allowed opportunity to take on human form possessing power, influence and authority. Mr. Opportunity held the keys to my future and there wasn't anything I could do about it. Sounds ridiculous doesn't it? I went there, and I am not alone.

I would have this conversation with myself over and over: "It is time. Yes, it is my time. I am absolutely sure. No doubts. It is my time. It is my time to receive an opportunity. Opportunity should be knocking down my door. I am prepared. No one could be better equipped and ready to step into an opportunity than me. Yes! Me! Me! Me! What is going on? This is not fair!"

How many individuals have felt this way? Countless.

Is Mr. Opportunity really guilty of some underhanded trick? Or is he the wrong party to accuse? Sounds silly now, but before I understood the power I possessed to chart my own course, I claimed myself a victim of Mr. Opportunity. If I could, I would have reported him to the FBI, CIA or any other institution that would convict him of multiple counts of robbery.

Imagine for a moment if Mr. Opportunity had actually been indicted for these crimes. Read the opening statements in the case of *The People vs. Mr. Opportunity* carefully:

Judge: This court is now in session. We are here today to hear the case of *The People vs. Mr. Opportunity*. As we know, the defendant has been accused of robbery. Prosecution, you may begin with your opening statement.

Prosecution: Ladies and Gentlemen of the jury. I come before you to prove that the defendant (Mr. Opportunity) is GUILTY. Yes, he is guilty of robbery. I will also show his actions have caused many to feel neglected and mentally abused. He represents himself as the creator of favorable circumstances resulting in limitless possibilities. When Mr. Opportunity knocks at your door, it could yield promotion, proposal, prosperity, profits and peace of mind to name a few.

The prosecution will show that this is an open and shut case. Countless individuals have patiently waited for Mr. Opportunity to no avail. Mr. Opportunity continues to pass by the door. He never slowed down. He just kept moving – leaving behind disappointments, shattered dreams and feelings of abandonment. On countless occasions, he has robbed individuals of their hopes, dreams and success for the future.

Let's take the case of Jane Smith. She is a college graduate with an undergraduate degree and a master's degree. She works very hard for her company. She stays late, volunteers for extra assignments and is a true team player. Most would agree she is a rising star in the organization. Her resume is excellent and her reputation is spotless.

Jane heard of an opening for a new supervisor position in her department. She had been preparing for this opportunity to come her way so she applied for the position. Unfortunately, she was not offered the positioned. She wasn't even invited to interview. What happened? Mr. Opportunity just passed her by. And may I add, this was not the first time.

Let's look at the circumstances of John Smith. John Smith has a dream to become one of the men of distinction in a prominent fraternity on campus. He has expressed his interest to several members of the fraternity and has met the GPA requirements. He has saved the funds required to join the organization and has prepared himself academically, mentally, physically and financially for this long desired tradition and opportunity.

Rush week, the week new recruits are introduced to the Greek organizations, came and went. John Smith was not invited to join the fraternity, nor was he invited to join any other fraternity on campus. What happened? Mr. Opportunity just passed right by

John's dorm room door. What was once a long desired dream now appears to be a nightmare.

The next victim is Susan "I am ready to get married". She had been in a relationship with the same fellow for three years. She has been faithful. She spent Christmas with his family. On several occasions, they talked about sharing the future. Unfortunately, the relationship stalled and the future father of her children turned in his keys and moved on. To her surprise, within a year of their break up, she heard of his upcoming nuptials. What happened? Mr. Opportunity did it again. Susan "I am ready to get married" has become Susan "Why not me?"

These cases represent a few of many cases where Mr. Opportunity did not knock. Yes, ladies and gentlemen, you must find Mr. Opportunity guilty on all counts! I rest my case.

Defense Attorney: I object your Honor. The prosecution is misleading the jury. It would be easy to blame Mr. Opportunity for one's perceived lack of an opportunity. Ladies and gentlemen of the jury, let's take another look at the "so called victims of Mr. Opportunity". First and foremost, opportunity was there for all – they simply failed to see it. How quickly they surrendered and believed things were over! Now they just offer excuses.

The case of Jane Smith not being invited to interview was clearly an opportunity to speak with management and human resources to determine what she needed to do to increase her chances for consideration. There was also an opportunity to reassess the situation and pursue other methods to achieve her desired goal of becoming a supervisor such as cross training, shadowing, leadership development programs and so forth. There also existed the opportunity for her to continue to build her *reputation*.

John Smith believed Mr. Opportunity was guilty of robbing him of his dream.

Opportunity is not dictated by our time frame. What's not to say that he was being considered for the next class of recruits? John should understand that there is still a chance to become a member of the fraternity. John had an opportunity to exercise some ***resilience***.

Lastly, Susan "I am ready to get married" is heartbroken over the loss of the man she hoped would be her husband and the father of her children. You'll notice that the relationship was over for a year before he walked down the aisle with his bride. Had Susan considered there is someone better out there for her? She would be better served to see an opportunity to focus on building real and true ***relationships*** rather than looking for a husband.

Ladies and Gentlemen of the jury, Mr. Opportunity is innocent of these bogus charges. Before blaming opportunity for not knocking, take a long look in the mirror. The real culprit may be staring right back at you. No excuses folks. Open your eyes! Opportunities abound and success is within your reach. I rest my case.

If you were the judge and jury, what verdict would you render? Innocent or guilty? It's time to close this case and any further thoughts of Mr. Opportunity possessing some power or authority. He is a figment of one's imagination. He is just a convenient excuse.

Confessions of a Recovered Pessimist

I confess there was a time when indicting Mr. Opportunity made perfectly good sense to me. Today, however, I have no doubt that opportunity was and is always present. Looking back, I heard opportunity knocking at my door but I denied entry because it appeared to be a potential problem, trouble or too much work to achieve success.

When opportunity knocked, the conclusions I drew were not always justified. It was strictly based on my perception. My conclusions may have been considered subjective. Real, imagined, subjective or justified, my conclusions were *very real* to me.

On other occasions, I believed I was denied opportunity or excluded because of my race, gender, associations or positions I had publicly taken. Maybe these assumptions were true. Or maybe it was a convenient excuse to justify my failure to receive what I thought I deserved. Living through each situation was my opportunity to learn patience, resilience and trust in what God had in store for me.

> **Let's be real!** There is nothing that exists upon this earth that can control your destiny or limit your success unless *you* allow it.

Succeeding Against the Odds

When you perceive that opportunity isn't knocking at your door, it may feel like a missed opportunity. Not necessarily so. When I was in high school, every junior had to see the guidance counselor to discuss his or her plan after graduating from high school. Were you going to college or planning to take up a trade? If you were going to college, what would you major in and how would your parents pay for it?

I recall being so excited about planning for my future. I just knew I would be a news reporter, an evening news anchor, talk show host and a White House correspondent. How I was going to be all those things, I have no idea. In my little mind, I just knew it would happen.

Well, my visit with Mrs. Jones is what I call a "game changer". (Her name has been changed to protect her identity.) She asked many questions and I had an answer for everything. However, my response to her last question changed the course of my history – or it at least made the journey a little longer. She asked "What do you want to be?" I said I would like to be a news reporter then an anchor. Before I could finish my list, she said: "Baby, you are going to have a hard time being successful if you choose that." Her next words were so clear, confident and direct that I have heard them in my mind throughout the decades since that day. Mrs. Jones said: "You do not have strong European features. Who do you know on the news that looks like you?"

The person I am today would have been prepared for that sort of rejection, but at seventeen years old, I was floored. Long story short, I accepted her well-intended, misguided advice and prepared to chart another course to became an electrical engineer. This may seem like a missed opportunity for both Mrs. Jones and me. She could have helped a young person understand that her dream might be difficult but not impossible. I missed an opportunity to believe more in myself than in the words of a person who only saw me two or three times a school year. Or did I?

I believe every experience, good or bad, is an opportunity if you choose to see it in that way. My experience with Mrs. Jones has given me countless opportunities to share the story of **"Succeeding Against the Odds."**

By sharing my story, I have the opportunity to encourage others not to fall into the trap of self-doubt or let others predict your future. Listen to yourself. Pursue your passion. You've got to believe it, to see it. Would I speak these words so boldly had I not experienced what most would call a missed opportunity? I doubt it.

Collateral Damage

I have had an interesting and rewarding professional journey that continues to this day. I started out wanting to be a White House Correspondent and, within minutes, I was pursuing a career in engineering. Over the next two decades, I worked with the same company and had the opportunity to work in various departments: power delivery, marketing, economic and community development, environmental affairs, public relations, customer service and divisions operations. I had the opportunity to learn so much and be exposed to things that I could have never imagined. Some of the experiences were welcomed opportunities; others I would have passed if I had a choice.

On one particular occasion, my department was not in step with higher leadership. I assessed the situation and could see where there was right and wrong on both sides. Unfortunately, several adults could not see past their personal agendas, communicate, agree to disagree and just handle the business. The older I get, the more I realize this is not an uncommon incident – nor is it limited to business. It happens every day in families, in the church, in government and on playgrounds.

Nevertheless, decisions were made that resulted in the reassignment of individuals, including me. Initially, it was a hard pill to swallow. Pride led me to believe I was "collateral damage". One minute, I had a load of responsibilities and a team of individuals reporting to me. The next minute, I was an individual contributor knocked off the ladder for bigger opportunities. Or was I?

Actually, the reassignment became one of the best opportunities of my personal and professional life. I enjoyed a fulfillment I'd never before experienced during my career. The situation had as much opportunity to be a success as a failure. Not recognizing it at the time, the position I lost had begun to affect me personally, spiritually, financially, professionally and physically. I have no scientific proof, but doing that period, I was diagnosed with cancer followed by shingles. Being reassigned was an opportunity to get my house in better order. The entire experience turned out to be one of the best blessings for my family and me. What an incredible opportunity!

My Daddy

I thought I was the chosen apple of my Daddy's eye. Being the "Baby" in a family of seven, I had a special relationship with my Dad. I can recall tagging along with him. Wherever he was, I wanted to be, too. When he replaced shingles on the roof, I was sitting on the roof watching him. When he worked on the car, I was the junior mechanic. If I heard his truck crank up, I ran out the door saying: "I want to go!" He was the perfect father in my eyes.

Then one day that all changed. I found out he was not "Father of the Year". He wasn't perfect. He had flaws. Yes, he provided a roof over our heads. Yes, he put food on the table. Yes, he went to church. And yes, he betrayed my trust.

There was a family secret. Everyone knew about it. No one spoke of it. I was told that was just what people did back in the day. But I wasn't buying it. I was ready and attempted to blow the cover off this situation. But I was met with opposition on all sides. It was a secret. Really? Just because you do not talk about something doesn't mean it is a secret or it didn't happen.

Believing he had betrayed me, I took it as a justifiable opportunity to withhold my love and respect from him. Simply stated, I became a brat. Brats are tolerable when you are age 2 or 3. But when you are in your twenties acting like a brat, trying to gain some form of revenge, it's beyond ridiculous. And it's shameful – sinful, actually. I can offer immaturity as an excuse, but it does not justify my actions.

As the saying goes, time heals all wounds. I carried a heavy burden of guilt, shame and judgment too long. I eventually took the opportunity to talk with my Dad, clear the air, offer forgiveness and express my love. I really missed some precious time in our relationship because of how I perceived the entire situation.

I am so thankful I took the opportunity to make peace with him and the entire situation before I lost any more time with him. Today my father sits in a nursing home suffering from Alzheimer's. It breaks my heart to see him suffer – it's like watching a slow death. Alzheimer's is such a cruel disease. I could have never predicted things would turn out this way. Betrayal or not, I would give anything to have my Daddy back – flaws and all. Needless to say, I have my share of flaws, too.

How ironic this example is to me today. In some ways I feel I am reliving the past except this time it is my husband, instead of my father. I believe that God prepared me for this period in my life through the events that occurred with my father. I learned many valuable lessons with how I handle my father. Today, I am applying those lessons as I am called to have Grace under Fire.

When things occur in our lives, we can never predict exactly how they will turn out. Approaching every experience as an opportunity to make the best out of the situation is a wise choice. Each of the earlier situations could very easily be considered a missed opportunity or a bad situation. But they weren't.

Speaking to groups on the topic "Succeeding Against the Odds" has been my opportunity to inspire and encourage students to pursue their passions. Considering myself as "Collateral Damage" gave me an opportunity to learn a very powerful lesson and a lot about my personal strengths. When you are knocked off of one ladder, get up and believe "It Ain't Over!" As for "My Daddy", his actions provided me an opportunity to understand what it means to love unconditionally and learn a hard lesson. As for "My Husband", he has provided me an opportunity to publicly explain unconditional love, to show God's Grace is sufficient and be reminded that all things work together for the good to those who love God, to those who are called according to His purpose. (Romans 8:28)

One should always make the best of every situation. You cannot make up for lost time. Yesterday is gone. Tomorrow is not promised.

What's Next? Spectator or Participant

Well, the ball is in your court. Actually, the ball has always been in your court. It was never over and will not be over until you breathe your last breath. We were created with a mind, abilities and free will. Failing to achieve or feeling limited has more to do with self than the environment and the influences in your surroundings.

In defense of those, including myself, who at one time or another failed to recognize the opportunities within our reach, I offer this theory. Operating in an environment that doesn't always appreciate or encourage individuality, confidence and determination tends to yield complacency. It becomes easier just to assimilate, stay in the box, keep your head down and *wait* for that opportunity to knock at your door.

Waiting for something to happen is a disservice to self. How long will it take until you realize you hold the keys to the door? There is a time for one to be born. There is a time for one to die. If we knew the day we would depart from this earth (die), I imagine we would take control of the pen and write our own story instead of leaving it up to chance.

If we knew exactly how long we had to live, maybe we would take every opportunity that came our way, create them, make the best of every situation and focus more on making a lasting, positive difference in the world. Not knowing the date leaves a false impression that we have forever – and so we take life for granted.

We were born to live. I don't consider waiting to hear a knock at the door *living*. Waiting is a poor excuse for not getting out in the world and creating your own opportunities, leaving your mark, succeeding on your own terms and living a more fulfilling life.

It's your choice. You can be a spectator and wait to see what happens next or you can be a participant, shape your own future and fulfill your destiny. If you choose to wait, know that you have made a choice and you must, therefore, _own_ the consequences of this choice.

What happens between your birth date and your burial date is all up to you. **It Ain't Over** until we receive the end date. Being able to think, have free will and to choose how you live is an opportunity in itself. Actually, it is the greatest opportunity. Not every person has this privilege. Some places around the world do not allow such freedom. I am very grateful to be a citizen of the United States of America. I am most grateful I can worship and serve a God that reminds me that all things are possible.

One opportunity can open a door, turn the tide or enable you to succeed against the odds. See the formula once again. Each factor individually can play an important role in influencing the chances for realizing an opportunity. However, if you work hard on building an excellent reputation, practicing resilience, cultivating relationships and believing in the resurrection, the opportunities are endless.

$$Opportunity = \frac{\underline{Reputation \times Resilience \times Relationships}}{Resurrection}$$

Now what?

It is all up to you. This book was written to encourage and raise awareness that **It Ain't Over!** I hope your reading has been time well spent. There should be no doubt in your mind that luck isn't what brings opportunity to your door.

It's all **YOU**!

TAKEAWAYS

1. At the intersection of opportunity and hard work is success.

2. The principles to increase opportunities include reputation, resilience, relationships and resurrection.

3. It takes a lifetime to build a good reputation and a second to tear it down.

4. There are benefits in learning what to do as well as learning what not to do.

5. The two most important relationships are the ones established with God and self.

6. Resurrection brings about revival, restoration, rebirth and resurgence.

7. Opportunity is always knocking. Your perception will determine if you hear it.

8. An opportunity doesn't always look like an opportunity. It could be undercover, disguised as a problem, waste of time or a nightmare.

9. The power to succeed lies within you. You have to believe it to receive it.

10. One should always take the opportunity to make the best of every situation. Tomorrow is not promised.

11. Until you take your last breath, "**It Ain't Over!**"

FROM MY MOTHER

It Ain't Over!

I am speechless as I consider what Joyce has accomplished in her life and through this book. She is a very smart person. People look at life through different lenses and I can see she has been looking within herself. I can relate to her words. When you have dreams that have not been fulfilled you should just keep trying.

Regarding reputation: if you get a bad reputation it's hard all the way around. Joyce has a good reputation and she protects it by living according to the Bible.

Regarding resilience: this is something Joyce truly understands. She has had some things she's had to live through and she always bounces back. Each struggle has made her a stronger person.

Regarding relationships: if you don't love yourself you can't love anybody else. I am glad she loves herself.

Regarding resurrection: there are traits needed for resurrection – honesty, faith, confidence and trustworthiness. I've seen these traits in Joyce as she has fought to overcome her own struggles.

If you are waiting for opportunities to come to you, get out and try. If you fail, get up and try again. You've got to rise above your failures because: **It Ain't Over!**

Hattie L. Pettway, mother of Joyce E. Brooks
Assisted by Shirley Sutterfield
September 2014

AFTERWORD

I've learned that people will forget what you said,
people will forget what you did, but people will never forget
how you make them feel. ~ Maya Angelou

I met Joyce in late 2013 at a leadership workshop for association professionals. Her topic, "Self-Inflicted Overload," was so timely and her personality so dynamic, I truly don't remember any of the other speakers from that particular day. In fact, Joyce's presentation was the first "motivational" session I'd sat through in quite some time where I didn't check my iPhone – not even once. Remarkably, neither did anyone else. For nearly an hour, Joyce kept our full attention. Her message was clear, engaging, humorous, inspiring and *authentic*. Joyce spoke *to* us, not *at* us. She made us laugh. More importantly, however, the personal challenges and triumphs Joyce shared were *relatable* – and allowed us to reflect on our own work/life situations.

I immediately recommended Joyce as a general session speaker for my organization's annual convention. I knew she'd be able to connect with a diverse audience and that her corporate background and motivational approach would captivate a sometimes difficult crowd. Of course, it's one thing to hold the attention of a small group for an hour; it's another thing entirely to serve as the closing general session speaker for 500+ local government leaders following three days of intense educational training. Joyce's energy and enthusiasm never faltered. In fact, her presentation, "Board Management and Effective Communications," was an unequivocal success. Attendees left laughing and smiling – with useful information that could be applied to real-life situations.

Following those two speaking engagements, an unexpected professional relationship and personal friendship developed. Joyce asked me to edit her latest book, *It Ain't Over!,* and offer suggestions. Little did we know at the time that this publication would become even more personal for Joyce. On May 28, 2014, following the sudden loss of her husband, soul mate and the father of her children, Joyce had to immediately begin structuring a new normal – not only for herself, but for her family.

It Ain't Over! went through a transformation as well – becoming even more vibrant … more earnest. Joyce channels her personal experiences in *It Ain't Over!* to illustrate that, regardless of race, gender, religion or socioeconomic status, we all experience similar, sometimes extremely difficult life challenges – and that how we move forward is up to us.

It was an honor to collaborate with Joyce on her latest endeavor; however, it was my good fortune to develop a friendship with this authentic woman I respect and admire.

Thank you, Joyce! **It Ain't Over!**

Carrie Banks
Communications Professional
Montgomery, AL
September 2014

BONUS

IT AIN'T OVER: THE SPOKEN WORD VERSION

Reflections by
Joyce E. Brooks

I Am Who I Am

O.K. Everybody. I am who I am.
And I am not apologizing for it.

Here we go again
At the cross roads of what "They" want and what
I deserve.
Being a minority has it advantages, especially when
You are use to it.
"The first", "The only", "No one has", "No one will"
Sounds familiar? That's me!
"The first", "The only", however I will.

Fueled by a burning desire to be me.
Stripping away labels, others' expectations,
Failing to conform
If I am not careful, "They" will have me believing,
Not only do I have a problem,
But I am the problem.

Guess what?
Didn't ask for your opinion.
Never expected to be accepted.
And I am fine with whatever the outcome
Because I am who I am.

Can't fit in the box. Love to think outside the box.
"They" really didn't mean for me to do it.
What? Think outside the box.
Not only am I out of the box, thinking outside the box,

I have conveniently misplaced the box.
You know. If you think about it, shoes are more
Appealing sitting on a shelf
Where you can see from heel to toe, from top to bottom.
If a few ounces of leather is more appealing
Without a box
I think my +/- 172 pounds can be as well.

Not angry. Not resentful. Not even pissed off.
To be absolutely honest,
I am disappointed and saddened that
"They" find it necessary to mode, shape, develop, retrain
And model me in order to exist.
Have you not heard?
I am created in His image.
How arrogant to think "They" would need to mend,
Alter or correct His creation.
But that is what "They" try to do.

Can't do it. Won't do it.
I am who I am.
+/-172 pounds of caring, passionate,
Strong, loving, surviving,
Brown, round and sassy flesh and blood.
Temperamental maybe. Energetic is more like it.
But "They" are not comfortable with all that reality.
Safer to see it on T. V.
Than to find it up in your three feet zone.

Hello, I am who I am.
And I am not apologizing for it.

Love, where are you?

Love, where are you? Speak to me.
Speak to me Love.
Oh, how I miss you. I am incomplete without you.
I am lost in your absence.

Love, where are you? Speak to me.
I am intoxicated with your power.
Humbled by your strength.
Safe in your presence. And satisfied when we touch.

Yes, My Love.
It is you – that gives purpose to my living.
It is you – that energizes me.
Converting my electricity from DC to AC.
From Direct Current with my highs and lows
To Alternative Current bringing me to the source of
Unconditional, everlasting, eternal love.

Love, where you are? Speak to me.
Am I deaf, blind or mute?
Have I lost my mind? How could I doubt you were here?
You have never departed me. Even when I had thoughts
of departing myself.

But no. You are here. Where you have always been.
Beside me, Behind me, In front of me and – Oh, yes –
In me.

Oh Love,
Forgive me. I am not without sin. I have no perfections.
But you look beyond my faults and see my needs.
And love me more, more, and more.

Love, speak to me.
Whisper softly. Show me you love me, again and again
and again.
Don't stop. Show me again and again and again.

I feel your love in my head, my heart, in every cell and
every nerve that makes up my body.

Love, I feel you in my spirit.

I feel those three little words I-LOVE-YOU flowing
through my veins like the Notes of a keyboard playing.
How Sweet it is to be loved by you.

Yes, My Love.
You are here. Where you always been.
Beside me, Behind me, In front of me and – Oh, yes –
In me.

How Sweet it is to be loved by you!

ABOUT JOYCE E.

Joyce E. Brooks is managing member of Brooks Consulting, LLC whose mission is to assist businesses and organizations gain a competitive advantage by focusing on individual, leadership and professional development. Joyce is also the author of *Self-Inflicted Overload: Five Steps to Achieving Work-Life Balance and Becoming Your Very Best* and soon to be released, *It Ain't Over! Three Little Words that Lead to Personal and Professional Fulfillment.*

Joyce started her corporate career over two decades ago as an electrical engineer at Alabama Power Company. Within five years, she was being groomed for leadership – working in marketing, public relations, corporate services, community relations, economic and community development, customer service and serving as area manager for the company's largest division.

Her career was on the fast track, but in September 2008, a breast cancer diagnosis forced Joyce to step back and reevaluate how she managed her time. She was juggling a lot of balls – professional, mother, wife, daughter, sister, friend, volunteer, church member, and the list goes on …

Joyce realized that her very best was being hindered by her overloaded schedule and lack of work-life balance. So when she was declared cancer free in 2009, she pressed the reset button and started implementing strategies to live a more balanced life. Joyce's new approach led her to start writing, painting and spending quality time with family and friends. Joyce was living a more balanced life and, in the process, she found PEACE.

Four years after her breast cancer diagnosis, Joyce stepped out on faith and decided to retire from her promising career to focus on her family and helping other professionals achieve work-life balance. That same year Joyce published her first book, *Self-Inflicted Overload*, where she shares the "PEACE Strategy" that guided her personal journey.

Joyce holds a Bachelor of Science degree in Electrical Engineering from the University of South Alabama and a Master's degree in Electrical Engineering from the University of Alabama at Birmingham.

Joyce lost her husband and soul mate of 14 years in May 2014. She is the mother of two boys, Jae and Matthew.

www.joyceebrooks.com

ACKNOWLEDGEMENTS

A sincere and heartfelt thank you is

extended to ALL for the prayers, support and

encouragement received in the writing of

It Ain't Over!